Leadership Styles Based On Team Effectiveness

Leadership from a new perspective

notionpress.com

Leadership Styles Based On Team Effectiveness

Leadership from a new perspective

D. S. Pandit

notionpress.com

Notion Press

5 Muthu Kalathy Street, Triplicane,

Chennai - 600 005

First Published by Notion Press 2015

ISBN: 978-93-5206-020-7

Disclaimer

All examples given in this book are imaginary. They are just a means to explain a specific point. If you find any similarity between these examples and any individual or organisation, it only indicates that the styles described in this book are very commonly observed in real life.

Acknowledgement

At the outset, let me express my gratitude to all those who made this book possible. I thank my *parents and teachers* for educating me. I thank all my *family members*. A special thanks to my *wife*, who has always been a dependable source of support and encouragement for me. I would like to thank everyone who has directly or indirectly contributed to this book.

I would like to thank the *publisher*, for helping me in reaching out to my readers. And finally, I must thank all the *readers* for sparing their precious time to read this book!

Regards,
D. S. Pandit

Contents

Introduction

Definition

In this book we are going to discuss leadership from a corporate point of view.

A *leader* is a person who *leads a team.* In a corporate environment, the leader is *expected to represent and guide a group of employees.*

Success Criteria for Leaders

For an employee, success can be measured based on their own skills and achievements. However, for the leader, the success criteria changes to the skills and achievements of the team he or she leads. In other words, the yardstick for a leader's success is the effectiveness of the team.

Example: Captain of a Cricket Team

To give an example, let's consider a cricket team. As a batsman (individual contributor), success can be measured based on how many runs he scores, with what consistency and run rate. But for a captain (leader), scoring runs or taking wickets alone is not success. The

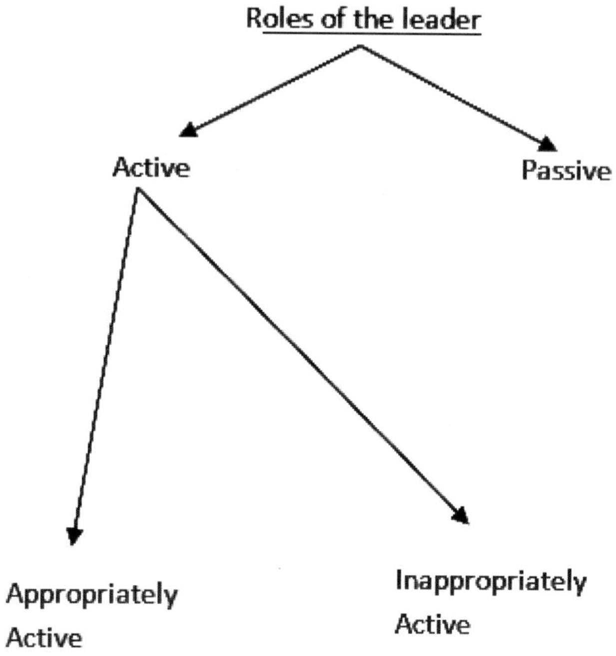

Fig 1: Roles of the Leader in Team Effectiveness

The following figure (Fig 2) shows the co-relation between the type of role played by the leader and team effectiveness. If the leader is *passive (does not put in any effort)* then the effectiveness is purely a function of the team's talent. If the leader is *inappropriately active*, then the leader's efforts are put in the *wrong direction*, leading to the team not being effective. If the leader puts more and more efforts in the wrong direction, team effectiveness is adversely affected that much more. If the leader is *appropriately active*, then the leader's efforts are put in the *correct direction*, leading to the team being effective. The leader's efforts in steering the team in the right direction enable team effectiveness.

In the subsequent chapters, we will be discussing each type of role and the leadership styles associated with that type of role.

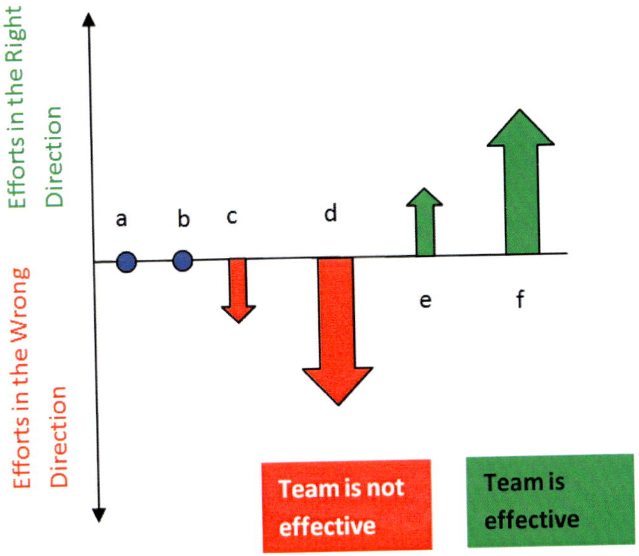

Circle indicates passive behaviour

Size of the arrow indicates the magnitude of effort and magnitude of impact it has on team effectiveness

Direction of the arrow shows if the efforts are in the right or wrong direction

a & b: Passive

c & d: Inappropriately Active

e & f: Appropriately Active

Fig 2: Efforts put in various types of roles and team effectiveness

Syles of the Passive Leader

A passive leader does not participate in the work. The team's effectiveness is not influenced by the presence or absence of such a leader. We can say that the team's effectiveness is '*irrespective of the leader*'.

Reasons for passive behaviour

- Lack of motivation
- Lack of knowhow
- In some cases, laziness
- Lack of time (a specific team not being the leader's priority).

Impact on the team members

- Some team members may feel helpless
- Some may become more responsible and take charge of the situation
- Team members may select an informal leader among themselves. But this leader will not have any formal authority
- The team will not have much respect for the leader

- Some team members will use this opportunity to enjoy and relax
- Indiscipline can crop up
- Some talented team members may get the desired freedom and be motivated.

Impact on team effectiveness

- Team effectiveness is a function of the talent of the team (not influenced by the leader)
- Weak teams will not be effective
- Strong teams can still be effective, but will not be able to perform to their full potential.

Probable outcomes of passive behaviour

- One probable outcome is that team effectiveness will be achieved, but not to its full potential
- The other probability is that team effectiveness will not be achieved, possibly, in spite of the team having the potential.

As we discussed initially, the success of the leader should not be measured based on his or her actions, but based on the effectiveness of the team. Hence for the same passive behaviour of the leader, we have the following two leadership styles depending on team effectiveness.

***

The first style for a passive leader is *'Forgivable Non-participation'* which is described below.

Forgivable Non-participation

Key characteristics

- The team is effective. However, it has much higher potential than what has been achieved
- The leader has no role to play in the success of the team.

Advantages

- Some talented team members get freedom, which is good for their growth
- The leader is not explicitly de-motivating the team.

Drawbacks

- The full potential of the team is not realised
- Less experienced team members are not mentored properly.

Although this is not an acceptable style, it is 'forgivable' because the team is still a winning combination.

Example: Forgivable Non–participation

In an organisation, a senior manager of the Operations department was given additional charge of the Technology team. The Technology team was working on designing the architecture of a new project. They were stuck on the decision of selecting the database technology. There was one technology which was very good and easy to support, but its cost was high. There was another open source option, where license cost was not involved, but support and skills for this database were not readily available and going with this technology might have risked the project timelines. Since this was an important strategic decision, the team wanted guidance from the leader. The leader expressed his inability, stating that he was not a subject matter expert. He told the team to decide to the best of their ability and take it forward. This is an example of a passive leader. In this example, to some extent, the organisation is also at fault for appointing a leader who does not understand technology. But the leader was so indifferent that he did not try to consult an external expert in order to help the team. Perhaps, he was very busy, or less motivated to contribute. Or may be Operations was his priority and Technology work was just another added responsibility.

In this case, eventually, the team, on its own, did some research and selected a good option that balanced both budget and schedule requirements and the project was successful. Since the team was effective and the leader was passive, this is an example of 'Forgivable Non-participation'.

***

The other style for the passive leader is *'Unforgivable Non-participation'*.

Unforgivable Non-participation

Key characteristics

- The team is not effective. It does not meet the targets. This may happen even if the team has the required potential
- The leader does not fulfil his responsibility. The leader's actions are needed for the effectiveness of the team, but the leader does not participate.

Advantages

- There are no advantages.

Drawbacks

- The full potential of the team is not realised
- Less experienced team members are not mentored properly
- The team can be de-motivated.

This is not an acceptable style. It is called 'Unforgivable' because the team could have won, had the leader done his or her job.

Example: Unforgivable Non–participation

A team was working on manufacturing readymade garments for a client. The client changed the branding and intimated leaders of all the outsourced teams about the change in branding and logo. The client also offered a walkthrough of key changes and requested the leaders to nominate team members for this walkthrough. It was mentioned that after a particular date, products with the old logo would be rejected. The leader of this team was passive/non-participative. He either did not understand the importance of this communication or its relevance to his team's effectiveness. As a result, he did not even forward the intimation to his team. Ideally, even the walkthrough was much needed. This resulted in rejection, rework and customer dissatisfaction. In that quarter, the team could not meet its target.

In this case, the leader was passive and the team was not effective. The team could have been effective had the leader done his job. The leader's passive behaviour can be blamed for the failure of the team. Hence, this is an example of 'Unforgivable Non-participation'.

Styles of the Inappropriately Active Leader

Inappropriately active leaders are participative; however, their actions are either in the *wrong direction or disproportionate.* An example of action in the wrong direction is giving more priority to trivial things and vice versa. An example of being disproportionately active is wanting to participate in each and every activity.

Team effectiveness is negatively influenced by such a leader. We can say that the team's effectiveness is '*in spite of the leader*'.

Reasons for such behaviour

- Insecurity. Fear of losing control
- Not learning to delegate
- Habit of micromanaging
- Poor time management
- In some cases, less maturity
- Not being able to look at the big picture
- Fluctuating priorities.

Impact on team members

- Experienced team members may get distracted
- Inexperienced team members may get misled
- Since the team is kept busy in unnecessary tasks, mainly to avoid hurting the leader's ego, they get frustrated
- Fluctuating priorities result in fatigue
- Team members do not get the required freedom
- Stress is created due to being under the microscope constantly
- Many team members are made to work on tasks without knowing the business context.

Impact on team effectiveness

- Teams with less experience will not be effective
- Talented and experienced teams will struggle, but they may eventually achieve the target
- Efficiency suffers due to overheads like giving frequent status updates to the leader or seeking frequent approvals
- There is a high likelihood of missing the big picture because the leader participates on the ground so much that no one gets the time to have a 10,000 ft view.

The first style for an appropriately active leader is *'Attempted Enablement'* which is described below.

Attempted Enablement

Key characteristics

- The team is not effective. However, it performs to its potential
- The team is usually less experienced or less skilled as compared to the targets
- The team leader performs very well, but cannot ensure the team's success. This is either because of very high targets or lack of adequate resources.

Advantages

- High motivation
- Team members get good knowledge and experience
- Team members respect the leader
- The Team enjoys a good working environment.

Drawbacks

- Team targets do not get achieved
- The team leader can be held responsible for the unavoidable failure and this can cause de-motivation for the leader.

This style is called 'Attempted Enablement' because, although the team is not effective, the leader makes a good attempt.

Example: Attempted Enablement

In a prestigious cricket tournament, a new, less experienced team qualified for the first time. They played well under the leadership of their captain. They reached the quarterfinals. It was a match where they were going to play against the defending champions. They won the toss, batted first and put together a formidable total. The captain himself scored a quick-fire half century. Their bowling attack was not strong. But the fielders fielded very well. The captain's field placement was so good that the defending champions were struggling to score runs. Finally, the defending champions won with 5 balls and 2 wickets to spare. The finish was so close and the match was so exiting, that the losing team won the hearts of the audience and all cricket lovers.

In this case, the leader had a tough target and limited resources. But he made a very good attempt. Unfortunately, he did not succeed. The combination of such behaviour and outcome is called 'Attempted Enablement' style.

***

The other style for an appropriately active leader is *'Successful Enablement'*.

Successful Enablement

Key characteristics

- The team is effective. Moreover, it performs to its full potential
- The leader plays an active role and contributes to the effectiveness of the team

- The leader is aware of the strengths and weaknesses of the team. The leader tries to exploit the strengths and mitigates the risks arising due to weaknesses.

Advantages

- The team performs to its potential and is effective
- The team is motivated
- The team respects the leader
- The team gets very good knowledge and experience
- The team enjoys a good working environment.

Drawbacks

- There are no drawbacks.

In this style, the team achieves its targets and the leader plays an active role in guiding the team to success. Hence this is called 'Successful Enablement'. This is the best style out of all the six styles discussed in this book.

Example: Successful Enablement

A poorly run hotel was taken over by its competitor. The new owners decided to retain the old staff, but appointed one of their star performers as the leader. He met the team and understood the strengths and weaknesses of the business. The strength was its convenient location. The problem areas were mainly outdated machineries like air conditioning, lifts etc. He drafted a makeover plan for the hotel and delegated most of the responsibilities to the team members and empowered them. The only two responsibilities that he kept with himself were the budget approvals and marketing. He convinced the new owners about the potential of the business and received approvals for investments in furniture, interior design and facilities. He also involved the digital marketing team of the new owner's company to maximise the hotel's publicity. During the peak season, he attracted additional tourists through smart campaigns. For lean periods, he entered into tie-ups with companies which required accommodation for corporate travel throughout the year by offering them good discounts. In the meantime, the employees completed the responsibilities assigned to them like repairs, replacing old machines and facilities with good ones, training the staff better in hospitality, quality assurance, etc. Thus the hotel's makeover and rebranding was complete.

His efforts resulted in improved occupancy rates and revenues. When the hotel was taken over initially, the staff was worried about their jobs. Just two years later, the unit was a profit centre which paid good bonus.

In this case, the team was effective and the leader played an active role which resulted in the success of the team. So this is an example of 'Successful Enablement'.

Ranking of Various Leadership Styles

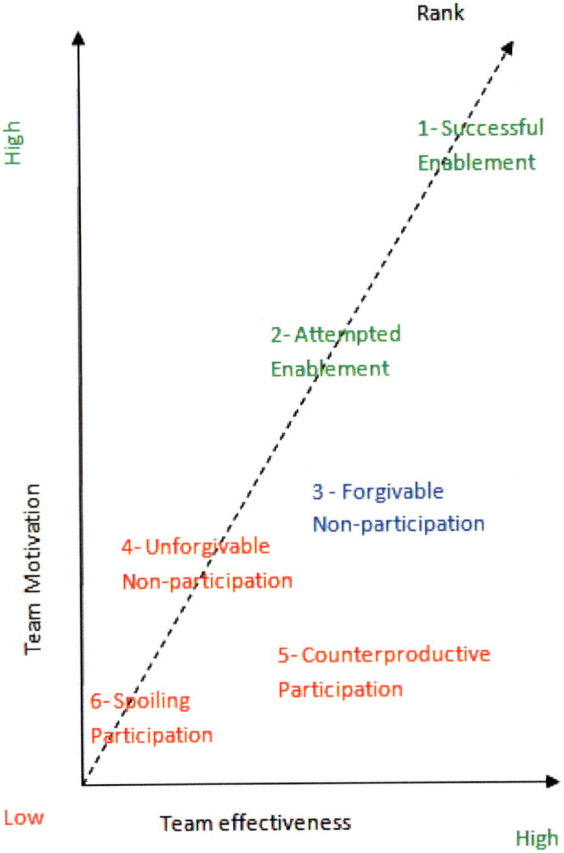

Fig 3: Ranking of six leadership styles

Figure 3 graphically explains the relative rankings given to various leadership styles.

A better leadership style results in higher team effectiveness and motivation. So, while ranking the styles, we plot them on the following two coordinates

- Team Effectiveness
- Team Motivation

The *worst style, no 6, is 'Spoiling Participation'*, which results in the lowest effectiveness and motivation. In this style, the target is not met, productivity is low and the team members undergo a lot of stress.

The *'Counterproductive Participation'* is a little higher in rank at *no 5*. In this style, the team is under high stress. Even though productivity and motivation are low, the team is able to achieve its goals. So this style moves ahead significantly on the team effectiveness axis and marginally improves on the motivation axis.

The *'Unforgivable Non-participation'* is the next higher in ranking at *no 4*. In this style, the team is not effective. One good thing is that the leader is passive and is at least not disturbing the team. The team is left alone to perform, based on its own talent.

The next higher rank, *no. 3*, goes to the *'Forgivable Non-participation'* style. In this style, the team is effective. The leader's non-participation is somewhat compensated by the team's talent. It scores moderately on both Team Effectiveness and Team Motivation parameters.

The runner up, style *no 2,* is *'Attempted Enablement'*. Although, the team is not effective in this case, the leader has tried his/her best. This results in less regret for the outcome. Motivation remains high. The Effectiveness score is also good because the team has tried up to its potential.

The *highest rank, no 1,* is given to the style *'Successful Enablement'*. In this style, both effectiveness and motivation are at their peak. The leader does exactly what is needed; nothing more and nothing less! It needs to be noted that in this style, the leader decides his or her actions in context to the requirements of the team and the target. For a less experienced or less skilled team, or for a very steep target, the leader decides to be more active. But for an easy target or while working with a very talented team, the leader will let the team do the needful and chose to be less active.

Knowing Your Leadership Style

In order to determine your style, you need to record some observations related to your leadership in one or more assignments. The *observations* need to be done on two parameters; *team effectiveness* and your *own participation.*

Team effectiveness related observations

Based on the targets set, note down if the team was *effective, or not effective.* The examples given in the chapter 'Effectiveness of the Team' will help you decide this. Another good way to determine effectiveness is *customer feedback.*

Observations about the leader's participation

Take your participation into account and classify it into one of the following

- Passive
- Inappropriately active
- Appropriately active.

Be unbiased and objective. Put aside your ego. If you do not have enough details for a past assignment, start collecting data for ongoing work for future use. It is a good idea to validate your findings with *feedback from your team.* Please keep in mind that team members will generally hesitate to give negative feedback to the leader. In some cases, lack of positive feedback in a certain area can hint at a negative observation.

Example: How to interpret the team's feedback

If a leader directly asks the team, "Do I micromanage?", then most of the team members will say, "No," because of either courtesy or fear. A more subtle way is to ask them, "What did you like the most while working on the assignment?" and, "What is the scope for improvement?" If a team member states that he or she received the required freedom, then it hints at lack of micromanagement. However, if a suggestion for improvement comes like, say, "The frequency of status meetings should be reduced", then it is a hint that you were probably micromanaging.

Here are some indicators which will help you classify your own behaviour.

Indicators of Passive Behaviour

- Had you taken leave every alternate day and if that would not have affected the work, then you were probably passive
- If the team approached you for help and you could not help in more than 60% of the cases, then it indicates that you were passive
- The team eventually failed but the team members

never approached you for help; then it shows that the team also thinks that you are passive and hence they did not expect a solution from you.

Indicators of Inappropriately Active Behaviour

- Frequent unplanned leave of the team members
- If you get status updates from all the team members directly, instead of from your direct reports
- You need status updates more often than once a week
- You participate in more than 50% of the tasks yourself
- You 'added value' by giving 'pro-active' suggestions to the team at least once a week
- The team was effective according to the customer, but in your opinion, it is a bad team and only because of your intervention, the customer expectations could be met
- The number of meetings arranged by you are at least three per week
- Action items of more than 30% of the meetings are not tracked to closure because other priorities come up during the year.

Indicators of Appropriately Active Behaviour

- Less unexpected absenteeism of the team members
- If the leader is on long leave, the team is looking forward to the leader resuming his duties
- The leader follows up about work with direct reports. Has only general chats with other team members
- Only in case of an emergency are meetings arranged

success for the captain is measured by how many times the team wins and with what consistency.

Comparison between Two Captains

As an exaggeration, let's consider two captains. 'Captain A' who scores zero runs in every match; but under his leadership, all the players perform so well that the team not only wins, but the team members appreciate the way this captain prepares the strategy, the batting line up, his motivating words on the field and in the dressing room, etc.

As against this, there is 'Captain B' who is an all-rounder; who scores runs and takes wickets consistently and is selected as 'the man of the match' in every alternate game. But the winning record of the team under his leadership is not good.

In this example, the leadership style of 'Captain A' is superior to that of 'Captain B'! This is because, the ranking is done based on the effectiveness of the team and not the abilities of the captain.

On the same lines, this book describes leadership styles and their rankings based on effectiveness of the team.

Hope you will find this book *interesting and useful.* Enjoy reading!

Effectiveness of the Team

KRA (Key Result Area) is a very commonly used term in today's corporate world. These are specific, measurable, time bound goals set for teams.

The following are some examples of such goals:

- Timely completion of a project
- Revenue targets
- Sticking to a budget
- Regulatory compliance
- Productivity targets
- Quality targets

Definition

Effectiveness of a team is the extent to which and consistency with which the set goals are achieved.

Examples: Calculating a team's effectiveness

Case 1: Missed all KRAs

Sr No	KRA	Importance / Weight	Achieved?	% Achieved
1	Revenue targets	50%	No	0%
2	Quality targets	30%	No	0%
3	Productivity	20%	No	0%
			Total	0%

Case 1 is an example of *very low* team effectiveness

Case 2: Missed important KRA

Sr No	KRA	Importance / Weight	Achieved?	% Achieved
1	Revenue targets	50%	No	0%
2	Quality targets	30%	Yes	30%
3	Productivity	20%	Yes	20%
			Total	50%

Case 2 is an example of *low* team effectiveness

Case 3: Achieved important KRA

Sr No	KRA	Importance / Weight	Achieved?	% Achieved
1	Revenue targets	50%	Yes	50%
2	Quality targets	30%	No	0%
3	Productivity	20%	No	0%
			Total	50%

Case 3 is an example of *moderate* team effectiveness. Even though the total achievement percentage is not satisfactory, the *high priority target is achieved.* So this is better than Case 2

Case 4: Achieved most KRAs including important KRA

Sr No	KRA	Importance / Weight	Achieved?	% Achieved
1	Revenue targets	50%	Yes	50%
2	Quality targets	30%	Yes	30%
3	Productivity	20%	No	0%
			Total	80%

Case 4 is an example of *high* team effectiveness.

Case 5: Achieved all KRAs

Sr No	KRA	Importance / Weight	Achieved?	% Achieved
1	Revenue targets	50%	Yes	50%
2	Quality targets	30%	Yes	30%
3	Productivity	20%	Yes	20%
			Total	100%

Case 5 is an example of *very high* team effectiveness.

Roles Played by the Leader

A leader can play an *active* or *passive* role in the effectiveness of the team.

Passive leaders do not participate and do not contribute to team effectiveness. Active leaders definitely participate in the work. However, if they contribute to team effectiveness in a positive manner, they are appropriately active, otherwise they are inappropriately active.

The types of roles played by the leader in team effectiveness will be clear from the figure on the next page (Fig 1).

Probable outcomes of inappropriately active behaviour

- One probable outcome is that team effectiveness will be achieved, but with reduced efficiency
- The other probability is that team effectiveness will not be achieved, may be, in spite of having the potential.

As we discussed initially, the success of the leader should not be measured based on his or her actions, but based on the effectiveness of the team. Hence for the same inappropriately active behaviour of the leader, we have the following two leadership styles depending on team effectiveness.

***

The first style for an inappropriately active leader is '*Counterproductive Participation*' which is described below.

Counterproductive Participation

Key characteristics

- The team is effective. However, it has much higher potential than what has been achieved
- The leader is active in the wrong direction or is indulging in micromanagement
- The team is good enough to withstand the interruptions and micromanagement, and still succeed.

Advantages

- There are no advantages.

Drawbacks

- The team gets pulled into unnecessary tasks due to pressure from the leader
- Productivity is low due to wasted efforts
- Stress is created due to close supervision by the leader
- Domination from the leader suppresses any good ideas from the team
- People at all levels are working on the nitty-gritty. This leaves no one to look at the big picture.

This style is called 'Counterproductive Participation' because the leader's participation is making effectiveness difficult, even though the team eventually achieves the target.

Example: Counterproductive Participation

A sales team in a bank was given the target of getting 1,000 new customers in a month. The leader was a perfectionist and wanted all the team members to plan their work thoroughly before starting. He insisted that the first five days need to be spent only in planning and analysis. Some of the team members wanted to hit the field as soon as possible. But they could not convince their dominating leader. Even after completing the planning, the leader insisted on daily status update meetings every evening, which all the team members were expected to attend without fail. In these meetings, they were questioned even if there was a small deviation from the plan. This was not only eating up one hour daily from the team's precious time, but was also inducing a lot of unwanted stress in the whole team. Eventually, the team managed to meet the target. But they had to put in a lot of overtime.

***

The other style for the inappropriately active leader is *'Spoiling Participation'.*

Spoiling Participation

Key characteristics

- The team is not effective. It does not meet the targets. This may happen even if the team has the required potential
- The leader's participation is excessively inappropriate
- The team is not able to overcome the excessive interruptions and micromanagement from the leader.

Advantages

- There are no advantages.

Drawbacks

- The team is not effective
- The team gets de-motivated due to being ineffective in spite of having the potential to succeed
- All the drawbacks of 'Counterproductive Participation' are applicable here also.

In the 'Spoiling Participation' style, the leader is dominating and micromanaging to the extent that the team cannot be effective. This is the worst of the six styles discussed in this book.

Example: Spoiling Participation

A company was into software development. One of the teams in this company had just completed an important project which was being tested by the customer for acceptance. The customer came back with seven issues which were fairly easy for the team to fix and secure not just a sign-off, but also win customer delight. Some team members were in favour of immediately fixing the issues and closing the project. But the leader did not allow the team to fix the issues first. Instead, he arranged a weeklong 'brainstorming' session to discuss the root cause of the issues. Finally he took a stand that the software was made as per the specifications and any modifications should be handled as a separate work order. This debate turned so ugly that the project launch was delayed and the customer scaled down the business with this company subsequently.

Styles of the Appropriately Active Leader

Appropriately active leaders are participative to the extent required, considering the work requirements and ability of the team. They add value by bringing in their expertise. But at the same time, they allow the team members enough space to grow and learn.

The team's effectiveness is positively influenced by such a leader. We can say that *team effectiveness is 'because of the leader'*.

Qualities that lead to such behaviour

- Good aptitude and maturity
- Collaborative attitude
- Good professional manners
- Rich experience and knowhow
- Focus and good time management
- Delegation skills
- Ability to look at the big picture.

Impact on team members

- The team is motivated
- Team members can learn and grow
- They get freedom and at the same time get guidance when needed
- The work environment is stress free.

Impact on team effectiveness

- Productivity is high
- Most teams are effective. In fact, some teams can scale new heights of success
- Some teams can still be unsuccessful (not effective). But these teams perform to their potential. If the team falls short, it is mainly because the target is too high as compared to the team's ability.

Probable outcomes of appropriately active behaviour

- One probable outcome is that team effectiveness will be achieved
- The other probability is that team effectiveness will not be achieved.

As we discussed initially, the success of the leader should not be measured based on his or her actions, but based on the effectiveness of the team. Hence for the same appropriately active behaviour of the leader, we have the following two leadership styles depending on team effectiveness.

***

more frequently than once a week

- Action items of most meetings are tracked to timely closure
- When the team seeks help, at least 60% of the times, the leader is able to give a solution
- Both the leader and the customers appreciate the efforts of the team.

Once you have noted down the values of the abovc two parameters (team effectiveness and your role in it), use the following table to know your style.

Let me once again repeat a word of caution that the leader should be true to himself/herself and put aside ego before determining the values of his or her behaviour.

Team Effectiveness	Leader's Behaviour	Leadership Style
Achieved	Passive	Forgivable Non-participation
Not achieved	Passive	Unforgivable Non-participation
Achieved	Inappropriately Active	Counterproductive Participation
Not Achieved	Inappropriately Active	Spoiling Participation
Achieved	Appropriately Active	Successful Enablement
Not Achieved	Appropriately Active	Attempted Enablement

Suggestions to Improve the Rank

For Inappropriately Active Leaders

If a leader is among the lowest ranking styles ('Spoiling Participation' and 'Counterproductive Participation'), the reason is Inappropriately Active Behaviour. In order to improve, the leader should do the following:

- The leader should scale down participation
- Have less frequent meetings on status updates and also have such meetings only with direct reports. Once a week is a good frequency for status meetings
- Delegate as much work as possible to the team and concentrate on what you keep with yourself
- Let the team members know that their ideas are welcome and consider any idea received with an open mind
- Let the direct reports know that they should approach you if they need any guidance or help anytime.

By doing this, you are likely to move directly to styles related to Appropriately Active Behaviour which are 'Attempted Enablement' and 'Successful Enablement'.

For Passive Leaders

If a leader is among the styles 'Forgivable Non-participation' and 'Unforgivable Non-participation', the reason is Passive Behaviour. In order to improve, the leader should do the following:

- While accepting a responsibility, consider your knowledge, experience, passion and available time. If you ignore these factors and take up an assignment for short-term gains, then you are taking the risk of becoming a leader with passive behaviour. A passive leader can only expect moderate success, if at all
- Try to have very talented direct reports if possible
- In case the direct reports have limited talent, try to hire consultants with subject matter expertise.

By doing this, you may not be able to become a very high ranking leader, but you should be able to meet the targets and maintain a good reputation.

For Leaders with Attempted Enablement Style

If you find that your style is 'Attempted Enablement', then the following tips are useful to upgrade to the 'Successful Enablement' style.

- This style indicates that the leader is doing well, but the team has some limitations. Try to add more talented team members if possible
- Also verify if the set target is reasonable in context to the resources available

- You mainly need to convince your senior management or customers to either give better resources or set reasonable targets.

If you are able to do so, you can easily reach the highest rank, which is 'Successful Enablement'.

In a Nutshell

The purpose of a leader is to ensure effectiveness of the team. Therefore, the success criteria of leadership style should not be centred around the attributes or actions of the leader himself. Instead, it should be centred around the effectiveness of the team.

If the team is effective 'in spite of' the leader, then it is a bad leadership style. If the team is effective 'irrespective of' the leader, then the style is passive. And if the team is effective 'because of' the leader, then it is a good leadership style.

To be classified into a specific leadership style, there is no fixed list of prescribed actions or attributes. The actions are in context to the available teams and set targets. You just need to do enough to enable the team to achieve its full potential.